Speaking Back

a new poetry anthology by the

Huntly Writers

Published 2023 by Huntly Writers (Huntly, Aberdeenshire, Scotland)
www.huntly-writers.org.uk

Publishing services by Lumphanan Press
www.lumphananpress.co.uk

Cover image: original artwork titled "Solitary Flight". Copyright Raoul
Middleman and used with kind permission of the artist's family

Speaking Back was collated and edited by Dawn McLachlan.

To contact poets individually please visit www.huntly-writers.org.uk to find
their biographies and direct contact details.

ISBN: 978-1-9996481-2-1

Printed by Imprint Digital, UK

*Selected poetry from members of the Huntly Writers &
past recipients of the Brian Nisbet Poetry Award.*

*Featuring work by Anne Manning, Annie Lamb,
Bernard Briggs, Cara Stevens, Carol Ann, Caroline Fowler,
Charis Connell, Dawn McLachlan, Donald Adamson,
Eileen Carney Hulme, Elizabeth McCarthy, Emily White,
Ian Atkin, Isla Martindale, Jennifer Rae, John Lamb,
Kerin Muir, Leon Stelmach, Linda Smith, Maureen Ross,
Molly Bashaw, Nick May, Nicola Furrie Murphy,
Patricia McParland & Scotty Mitchell*

Introduction

From a very young age we are told to stop "speaking back" and yet as adults we spend much of our time wishing we had more courage to do so. We know the importance of speaking back against injustice, harm, hate and the wrongs done by others. Throughout history poetry has been a powerful way of speaking back and speaking out.

We also literally "speak back" when we reach into the past and hear the words of those we have lost, or when we express that in our poems about them. This collection of poems carries an extra importance as we remember Huntly poets Patricia McParland and Brian Nisbet.

Patricia was a member of the Huntly Writers, and you can find some of her deeply moving poetry in this book. She left a legacy to the Huntly Writers in her will after her death in 2019 and it is that, in part, that made this book possible.

Brian was a much-loved poet and musician, and his loss is profoundly felt in Huntly since his death in 2015. You can find out more about Brian and his legacy at the back of this book, and you will notice that there are many recipients of the Brian Nisbet Poetry Award within this anthology.

Our cover illustration is a detail from a painting by the late Raoul Middleman who had a strong family connection to Aberdeenshire and the Huntly Writers. This painting – Solitary Flight – is a captured fleeting moment of our landscape and coast. We thank his family for kind permission to use this image for our cover.

In poetry and art we see mirrored reflections of our lives, locations, and the past and yet we also see out and through them like windows into the worlds and experiences of others. In this collection you will find us speaking back - and speaking out. You will find both mirrors and windows in poems of love, loss, life, legend, and legacy. Here we lay out our words in the hope that in these pages you too will find the voice to speak back.

Dawn McLachlan
Editor and poet – Speaking Back

Contents

*For Patricia McParland, Brian Nisbet
and Raoul Middleman*

You remain in our thoughts

Mask

The biggest lie we say every day,
Is in answer to the question,
"How are you"
"I am fine"

I hide behind a curtain,
A mask to hide my fears,
I block my pain receptors,
Push back all thoughts and tears,
Being joyful can come naturally,
And in truth being with others makes living,
Laughing, conversation and company,
Makes life more joyful and giving,
Still I tear away from prying eyes,
Sometimes others are suspicious,
My mask slips, people see through my lies,
I am left exposed and bruised,
Nonetheless, I can still be happy,
Despite all my pain,
Afterall, life is for living,
And there is so much more to gain.

Patricia McParland

Dehydration

When I am dehydrated,
I have the strangest sensation,
When I close my eyes,
All my limbs and my head,
Seem to grow to extraordinary sizes,
This has happened since childhood,
When I had a nightmare experience,
I was screaming down the hallway,
My arms growing uncontrollably,
Little did I know I was really,
Cradled in my mother's chest,
Sobbing wholeheartedly,
Believing my arms to be rapidly spent.

Patricia McParland

Thinking

I had a think about the thing you told me to think about,
I have come to a definitive conclusion,
From this I will not waver,
Now I have resolved it beyond all doubt,
An undeniable decision in which I am fully confident,
A new beginning, a new start,
But can I be so certain, sure of my own judgement,
A little hesitancy overtakes me,
Am I having a change of heart?

Patricia McParland

Change

A penny for them,
Spend a penny,
See a penny pick it up, all day long you'll have good luck,
Penny farthing,
Penny sweets or a penny black,
Penny slot machine,
99p a penny back,
We all require change
Clocks change as time goes by,
The earth revolves around the sun,
Daylight hours shorten or lengthen
Temperatures increase and dip,
Flowers sprout from seeds, blossom and wither
We all experience nature's bountiful variations.
The toys we used to play with,
Evoke happy memories with their simple delights,
The sweets we used to savour,
Bring images to life,
The places we adventured,
Provide glimpses of the past,
A history long over,
But not forgotten and will ever last,
We question whether modern children,
With their wealth of complex playthings,
Will experience and reminisce on times so fondly,
And the pleasures that they bring.

The fire roars and surges,
To fade to smouldering embers,
A spark reignites and burns ferociously,
To diminish and extinguish revealing cold coals in its wake.

Patricia McParland

Worship

We stand at the edge of our world,
camera snouts probing the space between,
waiting for a sign
from the far reaches.
"They come with the rising tide," she says.
A fin as sharp as desire
knifes the blue of the firth
and another and another.
an indrawn breath,
a pointing finger,
faces lit like stars.
Flukes flirt with the wind,
white water betrays
the despairing silver of a salmon
and the knowing smile of a dolphin.

Linda Smith

We Can See

we can see all the way
to the farthest light
fast to its rock
flinging its diamond smile

and in the morning calm
we'll see instead
its slightly shaky reflection
tacked to the air

through the day's mad whirl
often we spare no look
for the lonely pillar
gracing the far approaches

then twilight comes
with a beguiling wink
the dance is beginning
that will reel round all night

we have known rocks to split
pillars to fall
but in tomorrow's dusk
we shall be watching

Annie Lamb

This poem won third prize in the Brian Nisbet Poetry Award 2020

Visiting the Castle

We always made for the dungeon
scaring ourselves with the thought
of languishing in the dark,
wasting away – with no date of release –
on stale bread and water
or taken out and hanged.

Maybe what we feared
had entered us long ago
and echoed in the mind's dungeon
like the sigh of a ghost in our ear:
What are you, a prisoner or a jailer?
Would you turn the key?

Ach, we were only bairns
directionless as winds that souched
from north, south, east and west
around the battlements:
didn't grasp the conundrum
of the human spirit –

how blown this way, that way
by genes and dispositions
or birth or wealth
we still can choose our path
as turnkey, hangman, axeman or oppressor –
or liberator, letting in the light.

Donald Adamson

This poem was Highly Commended in the Brian Nisbet Poetry Award 2021

Urgent Message

Mother – here is the light of my eyes
darkened by the sight of broken buildings
broken bodies even of children   STOP

Mother – here is the opening of my ears
to the sound of bombs and shells
the explosions of fear and screaming   ST0P

Mother – here is the touching
Of my finger on the trigger, the
hammer of shame on my skin   STOP

Mother – here is the taste of blood
where I have bitten my lips my tongue
against these orders to kill   STOP

Mother – here is the smell of
the death of my soul unless I will
no longer do these things   STOP

Mother – I want to come back to you with
something other than blood on my hands   STOP

Maureen Ross

This poem was written on 24th Feb 2022 – the day Russia invaded Ukraine

Reverie

My grandfather told me of a forest
three days into the desert, reached by long march
and cold nights under an ice moon
with the endless sky of a billion stars
Restless and sleepless under dusty canvas
with drifting lilt of desert song
and bone-snap of a dying fire
he dreamt of home
Each morning they marched towards the distant shifting horizon
until the sun burnt air and lungs
Boots filled with hot sand and heavy pack pulling down
he marched on
leading until, in twilight, it rose from the sand
blackened ghosts of trees
claw-like branches scratching the blue belly of the approaching
    night
polished by wind and time
shining as glass
A petrified forest
casting lean moon-shadows against the rippled sand
a memory of life
a reminder of death

They marched on through
unsheltered by these parodies of trees
My grandfather broke step
to pluck a splintered fragment from the sand
Forty years later I sat
with a glassy fossil in my tiny hand
feeling it grow hot
a vision in my mind's eye of his past
and of one much greater
I hung on every word
seeing as clearly as if I had walked in his sand-filled boots
listening and dreaming
as my grandfather told me of a forest

Dawn McLachlan

This poem won first prize in the Brian Nisbet Poetry Award 2020

The Distant Sound of Bees

Nights I can still see my young mother
walk across her garden towards the field
as though across water, sinking through
as she bends to take something with her,
a weed, a potato bug. I wake with honey
stuck in my hair and go every day now
to that field, driving my music stand into
the soil, adjusting it like an antenna. But
she is done with words and has advanced
into the world. I have been meaning to
design a little flag for that place, a brown
silk-screened flag with a hill, a horse, three
stars, a squirrel. In winter I write her letters
in the first frost on my window, I melt the crystal ferns
with my thumbs, leaving spelling-bee words for her:
chrysanthemum, lily, ecophagy, hireath.

In the secondhand shop where she used to go
I stare into the window at an old-fashioned
sewing machine, imagine its needle singing,
imagine it sews the ground like a plow.
In summer I walk barefoot over the places
she once walked. And when the dogs on our street
lift their heads to howl or bark, I lift mine with them,
though it is just the rain coming down toward
our faces, the rain relenting again, opening
its doors to us as though we had knocked, as though
we were holding our hands out to it.

Molly Bashaw

This poem won first prize in the Brian Nisbet Award 2018

Organic Wine

Her final kiss was a spider.
Sometime she feels it still
Bumping soft and gentle
Against her waiting lips.

It nearly went inside her
just a leg slipped in
before she put the glass down
and changed her drink to Gin

Emily White

Lost Vision

I couldn't read words on the TV
My hand went to my face
No specs!
And not in the usual place
On the mantelpiece.
Then I remembered
Close work in the garden
Thinning out the beet
I had pushed my specs up on my head.
I went out in the twilight
Searched between the rows.
No specs.
Same thing in the morning, despite full light
I would have to go without.
I hadn't gone a whole day without
Since I was twelve.
(It's a long time, so don't ask!)
Would I see the number on the bus?
Would I recognise my friends?
I might go deaf for lack of moving lips,
Faces just a blur.

But I struggled through
Caught the bus, fulfilled commitments,
Listened carefully to what was said.

That evening my husband went out weeding
Found something strange in a bundle of green
And my vision returned!

Cara Stevens

Northern Summer

We ran into the waves
diving through surf,
the inevitable jolt
as we become wrapped
by the cold liquid cloak.
Through salty eyes
I catch your smile,
your carefree laugh,
my arms outstretched
to draw you close,
seagulls and terns swirling
against grey skies
with blue pockets
Afterwards,
skin tingling and wind whipping
our salt laden hair,
we skip hand in hand
as parent and child,
towards gritty sandwiches
on tartan rugs,
the sun still high
over this place
with countless memories
of timeless routines
on a Northern Summer's Day

Anne Manning

Normandy *(for Len)*

The landscape around us bears only subtle scars now
Decades have passed and grass smooths the fields once more
Soft breezes now carry only the sweetness of mown hay
And the distant breath of the sea
I think of him arriving here in that ruined summer after the war
With the earth still torn wide and stained with blood
Shattered towns and people
Long roads that had lost all signposts
And gained the tangled mess of an army heading for the coast
Marching until the land ran out
When he was last here the ditches and roadsides were
    incongruously decorated
Small red flags an improbable jollity
Splintered boxes and packaging smeared with white paint
Marking the shallow graves of those who did not make it home
The sheaf of officer's notes describing places no longer
    recognisable
In the faint hope that these lost sons and fathers could be
    recovered
They searched that hopeless summer, and into the seasons that
    followed
As nature already began to reclaim the wreckage of France
Orange blossom blessed the air
from lone trees that had once stood in village squares
Stray sunflowers reached up from fields that once glowed on
    hot afternoons
In one stretch of road an avenue of lindens stopped them in
    their tracks

The bees drunk on the only pollen for miles and miles
Filling the air with a soporific hum
The Earth carrying on
Life reaching for the blue sky from beneath the twisted wire
and metal
As we follow these roads now
Dappled light on stone farm buildings surrounded by rolling
fields
Laughter in the car and the warm conversations of a child and
their grandfather
Above, swallows and swifts now perform aerial feats in place
of war planes
The land has recovered but, in his eyes the wound was far
from healed

Dawn McLachlan

This poem won second prize in the Brian Nisbet Poetry Award 2022

Merry-go-round

Round and round and round and round,
The merry-go-round goes round,
Are you sick of it yet?
The merry-go-round,
The merry-go-round go round,
Never slowing, nor stopping, nor starting,
Just going round and round,
The lights are flashing,
The music playing loud on this haunted merry-go-round,
The horses you ride go round and round,
On this merry-go-round go round,
Their faces frozen in fear,
On this haunted merry-go-round,
Do you want to get off my dear?
Off this merry-go-round,
No luck you'll have stopping its spin, never forwards nor
    backwards and no begin,
The second those lights flickered on when your world begins,
Sometimes you enjoy the ride, sure,
But then you realise, there's no way off, no way to stop,
On this haunted merry-go-round,
Sometimes faster sometimes slower, sometimes almost still,
    sometimes spinning so fast nothing but wind passes,
But as the merry-go-round goes round goes round the lights
    begin to flicker,
Bulbs will break, horses will crack and the music starts to skip,
It starts to slow this haunted merry-go-round,

Goes round, goes round, goes round,
Then the lights will fade and the music will stop and the
    horses they will degrade,
But get off you can't for today is the day,
The merry-go-round stops.

Kerin Muir

Tables

Memories are laid like tables in my mind
Stacked against each other in the corners
Folded away and stored until needed
And then pushed together with the bright cloth of festivity
    covering the gaps
Unstable tables with the scars and wounds of years
Disguised by the trappings of the season
Imperfections, hasty repairs, and wonky joints no longer visible
Beneath the fresh spills and glorious clutter
Tables that we played our games upon
And laughed over
And shared the warmth and noise of each other in the coldest
    of times
Tables that grew smaller with each passing year
Fewer seats required
Faded cloth now overhanging our empty edges
In our memories
They are all still seated at my table

Dawn McLachlan

Only the Sun

Only the sun warms through
to the core of me
a fire's hungry flame
a rusted radiator bleeding heat
a snap-it hand warmer hidden
pocket deep
comes nowhere near
even to pale yellow
white sky days or
rays sneaking past
cloudy days
and
when she is nowhere in sight,
the memory of her
warms me still.

Anne Manning

Lindens

Don't tell me here
Not under the linden trees with the sky fresh and blue
and the whisper of the wind in the leaves
that draws in the summer clouds
like the day that came too swiftly to an end
Not while I can still feel the sticky sap knotting my hair
from the day the leaves were our umbrella
the rain glossing our cheeks and glistening our lashes
Not while the bees still hum their soporific tune of summer
    contentment
Don't make my memories of this rise up every time
the air is honeyed sweet with this blossom
Don't make me remember this moment every time
I walk this road
Tell me in a forgotten corner of a car park
Where even the feral dogs do not come
Tell me in a place that I will never revisit and never miss
Tell me anywhere
But don't tell me here

Dawn McLachlan

King Zephyr

The strains of 'Autumn Leaves'
Blown softly through bamboo reeds
While gentle touch of brush on skin
And mellow bass lines underpin
The tension and release

In cellar bars and smoke filled rooms
We swing and sway to tortured tunes
Reborn each time that they are played
The mould thrown out, the song remade
With altered harmony

Through whisky glass and smoky haze
I see King Zephyr stand to play
And he could fly on wings of sound
While I, feet firmly on the ground
Just play the Walkin' Blues

King Zephyr had a different sound
And every night a different crowd
For Jazzmen live to improvise
Each line a twist, a new surprise
Each night a different dawn

John Lamb

Keepsakes

Not her marcasite watch
or her favourite handbag
but two casserole dishes
and a patterned plate,
perhaps her life as a cook
influenced my choice
perhaps she'd smile
nearly thirty years later
to find me washing
and drying with care
these kitchen items
as the radio plays,
the sky on fire
this evening dizzy
with snowflakes,
memories melting on my tongue.

Eileen Carney Hulme

This poem won second prize in the Brian Nisbet Poetry Award 2021

Grief

How silently soft teardrops fall
Upon my weary ashen face
How quietly too the spoken word
In shreds like tattered antique lace.
Hushed translucent veil of whispers
As you enter every room
The heavy heart you cradle
Shadows dancing twixt the gloom.

The thundering roar of life's great ocean
Relentless, unforeseen
Raging storms crush anguished soul
Strangely calm, oft times serene.
Warm memories echo aimlessly
Tumbling through my muddled mind
Life's twisting thorny pathway
Stumbling blindly, undefined.

What is this cold dark dismal place?
Sense of loss so overwhelming
Jagged fibres flood my body
Engulfed by ceaseless trembling.
Stark sheerface of a mountain side
Abruptly paralysed my way
Was this His will, the chosen path
Or Mother Nature gone astray?

Caroline Fowler

Grace

Hands with black hairs, white skin.
Grab strongly and hang on.
They got bashed in training for the Goalball team.
They listen to the floor through the cane.
They flick over the face of a watch
and find the time.
They read sonatas in a crowded train
and flutter over finger holes of cherrywood,
decline the hand-hold of recorder books –
they do their own thing. (Double-jointed
and faster than possible, butterflies tune in to this music.)
They curl around a scalding cup of tea,
and pulled the canoe through the Wye rapids,
spinning it into the side – so much stronger
than the other paddle's hurrying hands –
Bang! And the river full of your laughter,
and mud from the bank.

These hands. Broken and mended many times
in the name of goals saved and won.
Paralympian for your country, father for the parish.

These hands lift her to where you know the mirror hangs
And you both laugh as she sees herself –
Laugh and laugh.

Emily White

This poem was Highly Commended in the Brian Nisbet Poetry Award 2020

Coral Pink *(for Rose)*

The house felt smaller the day after you surprised us for the last time
Two up
Two down
Small boxy rooms cluttered with a lifetime's collection
Of all that the seaside shops of the 50s had to offer
We stepped lightly into spaces that had never known silence
Until now
In the garden the huge apple tree cast its blossom whitening the
    grass like snow
Its branches blocking the light from reaching inside
I stood at a kitchen sink filled with crockery because you'd just
    stepped out
A short trip to visit him in the hospital
Then you'd do the dishes when you came back
On the table a half-drunk cup of tea on a mismatched saucer
There was the last trace of you on the rim
Coral pink

Dawn McLachlan

I Can't Breathe

The air's not what it used to be,
Nothing like it is now.
Now it's filthy and polluted,
And everybody wonders how...

The humans discovered something,
Something they thought was absolutely great.
But it's our darkest enemy now,
It's something us animals hate.

My fellow sea friends are trapped and wrapped,
The seaweed is poisoned and bad.
The sea is heaving with plastic,
It really is heartbreakingly sad.

Us wildlife eat it by accident.
We think it is something good.
We eat it and get horribly sick –
How do we know if it's food?

Humans made plastic and loved it.
They used it in all their tools,
Then burning it into the air,
What a bunch of fools.

Speaking of air, it's filthy.
See those cars that humans drive,
They send us into hiding,
And destroy the things that thrive.

They knock us down and hurt us.
They pollute the air as well,
There's billions everywhere; all the time!
They follow you wherever you go.

They cut down our delightful forests.
Taking away the trees and air.
For their own selfish matters,
It just isn't fair

And finally they lock us up in cages.
They test chemicals on our skin.
They take away or food –
And let us become really thin.

So let me ask you a question.
Do you think this is ok?
Because I am an animal
And I can't breathe.
But I hope to one day.

Isla Martindale

This powerful poem about the environment won the 2022 Brian Nisbet Poetry Award for a poet under 14 years old. Isla is an emerging writer based in rural Aberdeenshire. In her spare time, she enjoys walks in the countryside with her dog, doing arts and crafts, and playing her violin. When she leaves school, she plans to go to university and to travel around the world.

Choices

Fyles choices that we mak throu life
Kin aft times gar ye greet
Fu weel it's kent we shape oor sheen
Wi oor ain twa bauchled feet.

Stravaiged mony dreich low roads
Heich mountain taps hiv climbed
Syne, quairtly aince mair reminisce
Cassen weary een o'er time.

Yestreen fan I wis jist a bairn
Saft gentle Simmer breeze
Gran hoosies biggit doon wild wids
Yirdit knees scoort, sclimmin trees.

Ye learn'd real faist, fit's richt, fit's wrang
Noo choices... up tae you
Dour halflins aft times blurt things oot
Neist wi age, ca tee their mou.

Yont carefree days seen hytered by
O'er-vrocht thochts in a snorl
Whaur choices taen richt oot yer hans
Fegs... a contermashious worl.

Stravaiged mony dreich low roads
Heich mountain taps hiv climbed
Syne, quairtly aince mair reminisce
Cassen weary een o'er time.

May ilka day be stapp't wi cheer
An here's tae fit's aheid
Hud dear yon choices that ye mak
Canna tak them fan yer deid.

Caroline Fowler

This poem won first prize for a Doric poem in the Brian Nisbet Poetry Award 2021

Circular Truth

My mother told me
I must never tell lies
And I believed her.
But psychologists say
That seventy per cent of us lie
Ninety per cent of the time,
Yet ninety per cent of us
Always believe
What we are told.
A mismatch is apparent.
We lie, yet assume others
Are telling the truth.
We are both gullible
And deceitful in turn.
I still value truth
And seek it out,
Ask for evidence
To support any claim,
But if we aren't truthful
In our output
How can we demand
Truth in return?

To my children I say
Nobody likes finding out
They've been lied to.
You must never tell lies.

Cara Stevens

This poem won first prize for a previously published poem in the Brian Nisbet Award 2019

Chess Pieces in Dachau

I see your craftsmanship inside the glass.
Each stroke the blade made you chose with care.
I see you chose a general shape of square
but curved the chests of knights and noble heads.
The Queen is topped with such a perfect sphere!
To form that curve with just an eating knife
whilst holding on to the desperate thread of life
in here, where men wanted death and filth and fear
for you. I can see the focus of your gaze,
your hands, turning each one, to match the size.
There is nothing of the things they made
you do, in this glass case - exquisitely displayed.
Just you, unnamed unknown prisoner, who
I take home. Artist, I see you.

Emily White

This poem won first prize in the Brian Nisbet Poetry Award 2021

The Broadcaster

In a memory so dim it is
Hardly distinguishable from dream
My grandfather strides steadily towards me
Across a harrowed field.
On one shoulder is a bag
His other arm moves back and forth.
The rhythmic rasp of machinery
And the hiss of flying seed
Is this bow's music.
I hold up the flask and he stops
Thanks me, unscrews the lid
Takes one sip of the hot liquid
Sets it in the hedge for later.
This is the last time he will use the caster
Not because it is outdated (which it is)
But because he will soon retire.
He will sell this field
Plant only in his garden
And never sow another meadow.

Cara Stevens

Autumn has no fear

it sees the dark winter coming
and knows its beauty.

You bow your head down.
Gone – a dance of vanishing.
Just a black drop falls –

I plough your blood in,
the salt wet soil is dark
and the crop ripens.

Emily White

A Minstrel Passes

I have no song for summer
for dawns ignited in the afterglow
no song at all
nor any song for spring
for coral-tinted leaf and heron's call
no, none at all
but winter used to sing me
a cradle-song of speckled silver nights
she would recall
the harmonies of autumn
of tardy bees in flowers full of sun
and over all
the summer-heavy beeches in their wall
of storied shadows: for their treasury
no maker is too small

Annie Lamb

Barnard Castle

Bold above the river crossing,
A Plantagenet fortress rules still,
keep and moat and tower
looming dark over the town.
By the dry bones of a window
broods the sign of the Boar,
tusks trailing blood.
Shiver at the clash of pike and lance
in the gunpowder wind from the north

But this day in grassgrown ruins
Find a speedwell hidden,
fallen fragment of a fading summer sky

Linda Smith

Afterimages

I open the box
take out the ring, copper
baroque, place it on my finger
watch it absorb, reflect.

From the Uffizi to Palazzo Pitti
renaissance fills my heart.

Next to Dante's house I see
your bicycle hanging upside down
on an outside wall, that tiny apartment
where no surface appeared flat,
as a sliver of sunlight
tricked its way in.

With a disposable camera
I photographed our life.

Your artwork, my words,
a fusion of sacred, like drinking
water from the fontanelli, frescoes,
piazzas, bridges and cloisters
a medieval maze
of shimmer and shadow,
all that dreams declare.
Stay you said, the ground
trembling as each shutter closed.

Eileen Carney Hulme

This poem won second prize in the Brian Nisbet Poetry Award 2020

Avebury

Morning in Avebury.
Sheep stalk the stones,
a dishevelled crew,
pungent, yellow of eye
sheering each blade of grass
with irreverent precision.

Walk now the waiting stones,
circle, cove and avenue,
telling the pattern of their days.
Behind a shadow follows,
a thin susurration, a thrum
along the sinews of my heart.

Reach out, hold fast
to the bony fingers of the past.
 Listen, whispered the teller of tales,
here we danced the way of the stones,
here beneath the stars we loved,
and here we died.

Linda Smith

Autumn Evenings in Palmer Cove, Macduff

The view from his rock
Was as he had always known it.
There the gulls would scold and mock
But he didn't heed them. He would sit
And watch the water on harvest moon nights.
The sea below him would turn to foam
On windy evenings and he'd see the lights
Of boats as they made their way home.
Out in Banff Bay the lobster boats
Would chug up and down while
Fishermen in yellow oilskin coats
Sometimes waved... and he would smile.
The view from his rock
Was as he would always want it.

The view fae his rock
Wis as he hid aywis kent it.
There the gulls wid skirl an mock
Bit he didna heed them. He wid sit
An watch the watter on hairst meen nichts.
The sea ablo him wid turn tae foam
On winny evenins an he wid see the lichts
O boats as they mak their wiy home.
Oot in Banff Bay the lobster boats
Wid chug up an doon while
Fishermen in yalla ileskin coats
Sometimes wid wave...an he wid smile
The view fae his rock
Wis as he wid aywis wint it.

Scotty Mitchell

This poem won the Doric prize in the Brian Nisbet Award 2018

Buckie Luggers

Come awa fisher laddies, an come awa wi me
Wi oor six man crew, tae the caul North Sea
It wis Scaffies we sailed in the 19th century
They were kent as the wee Buckie Luggers.

Noo we fish'd e Moray Firth, tho wis aye in sicht o lan
Wi twa masts an a mizzen an a dippin lug tae han
Nae deck or nae shelter, easy hale't on saan
They were kent as the wee Buckie Luggers.

Wives nae mair cairrit men, for tae keep sea-hose dry
Aye, the boats bigger noo, partly deck'd forby
Nae langer beached, bit herbour'd nearby
They were kent as the wee Buckie Luggers.

Fae the mid-aichteen hunners, the Fifie wore the croon
Muckle sails gart gweed lick, canny furl't aroon
In the herbour were crammed, in their ain hame toon
They were kent as the wee Buckie Luggers.

William Campbell fae Lossie, he wis tae find fame
For he ca'ad tee a boatie an the Zulu wis its name
Iss craft sailed fast, fish'd further oot fae hame
It wis kent as the Ultimate Lugger.

Baith the Scaffies an Fifies were rummelt noo as ane
Wi a stracht bow, an steeply rake'd stern tee wis taen
Oot o aa the Herrin boats, iss een stood oot on its lane
Twis the Crème de la Crème o aa the Luggers!

Noo the Zulu wi it's sails o three, a radical design
Wi a dippin lug, a standin lug, twis jist anither kyn
Wi a mizzen an a jib, herrin met their hinnereyn
That's the tale o the aul Buckie Luggers.

Come awa fisher laddies aye an come awa wi me
Cast yer memories back tae yon caul North Sea
For these boaties are pairt o wir Scottish history
They were kent as the wee Buckie Luggers.

Caroline Fowler

At Findlater

Up here on the cliff
In the midpoint band of sea and sky
Where stone bleeds the collected heat of day into our hands
And the buttered coconut scent of gorse smooths the breeze
you
and I
rest
Here we sit
where rocks laid by men cling to rocks laid by time
For now, the advance of night is held at bay
by the syrup-light of sun's descent
trickling in its slow progression across the hills
Above us storm petrels outrun the bruised horizon
Below terns stitch the approaching tide with crimson bills
The first needles of rain prick my cheek
"Shall we?" you ask and hold out your hand
Your words snatched by gusts and tossed skylark high
"Not yet," I say
"Not yet."

Dawn McLachlan

The Rocks of Solitude, Glen Esk, Angus

In Spring, when the trickle of snow melt turns into a torrent,
    the waters of the North
Esk thunder their way down Glen Esk towards the sea.
Like an angry, charging beast the river roars and rears over
    rocks at a furious pace,
Tossing trees around like twigs in foaming turmoil.
Through the steep confining cliffs of the Rocks of Solitude, it
    continues its
Precipitous way.
It snorts out spume which fills the air with mist,
That rises and settles in droplets on weeping birches,
        Only to fall again like tears shed for the souls of
Napoleonic prisoners of war, who plunged to their deaths
        In this awesome, beautiful place.

Jennifer Rae

Hush *(for the Forvie Witches)*

This land was ours
Our blood ran deep and flowed hot through the bones of this place
First it was in whispers they denied us
We three who were one in covenant bound
thicker than the waters of the womb
closer than the swallowed blood of faith
We three craved only peace
and space
and the honest calm of this, our place
Soon their voices rose in jealousy, or fear
ignorance
intolerance
They found their volume in ale or kirk
and the voices rose and ignorance festered into hatred
From town to kirk they came in droves
crowded and seating in their crammed pews
strangling our truths and crowing falsehoods
They roared their fear
and would not afford us peace
Red in face and lumbering gait
they shut us out to cast our fate
We who walked quiet and barefoot on the sands
with salt-streaked hair and faces turned to sky
We who gathered eyebright for village maids
and bittersweet for pains of birth
and balms for aches and salves to ease the pain of grief

Those who once turned to us, now turned away
None defended us as they tore into our home
our small voices crushed by their anger
with their fear came deafness to our pleas
Forced into an aged fifie
clinker-built and planking split by time and salt
they cast us into the unforgiving waves
As icy waters lapped our hems
we clasped each other tightly as sisters do
and we cursed them then
We joined with the wind that tore at the shore
and our curse silenced all
We swept the land with sand
that swallowed all
house
kirk
noise
until all was a pure and wild silence
only the whispering of the shifting sands remained
our eternal command
hush...
hush...

Dawn McLachlan

Saint Andrew

where is our long ship
where does she lie?
where the fat cod feed
at the tail of the bank
where her back broke

what are these pale hills
plumes to the sky?
they are sisters
to the salt shoals
they are landfall

and what are those lop-winged birds
the great one trailing his legs
small shriekers scattering with the foam
would I know them
if I were flesh and bone?

my brawn and my bone
the wind in my beard
nose full of crushed pine
carnal white roses
crowberry, toadstools and snow

where is my beard now?
where do I lie?
under the warm dust
a faraway grove
where the doves cry

what of these poor bones?
how can they serve
you, lovers of Christ
in your wanton land
in the wind's eye?

Annie Lamb

Scotland my Home

Hear me,
Guide me,
For I have grown blind,
Through the moors,
The marsh,
Over the hills and snowy peaks,
Through this harsh land and into the forests I shall seek,
Guide me through these circled stones,
Through these ancient fires I feel in my bones,
Through the meadows which once stood here,
To the sand ever shifting and your rugged coasts battered by
    raging seas,
For Scotland has hope,
For Scotland is Home.

Kerin Muir

The Ski-Lift

Lookin throu auld photaes, a waa'k doon mem'ry lane
Seems like only yesterday, fin happy times were haen
A day oot in the Hielans, up the bonny Cairngorm
The ski lift wis the answer, baith legs dangling, free, airborne.

Twis fin hurlin on the chairlift, enjoyin the panoramic view
Ma mither startit lauchin, false teeth flew oot her moo!
She jist lauched aa the harder, michty me she cwidna stop
The altitude wis afa heich, neist thing her lugs did pop.

Takkin aff her glesses, tae dicht twa wattery een
She accidentally drapp't them, gone, naewye tae b' seen
Rumlichin throu her handbag, she raiked for her spare pair
Aathin coupit oot, an losh b'gosh gied fleein throu the air!

Camera, keiys an polo mints, hankies, kaim an purse
Plaisters, scissors, safety preens, cwid things get ony worse?
Clamberin fae her transport, she winted tae rin an hide
The Ptarmigan gied shelter, at top speed she nipped inside.

She cwidna see tae kaim her hair, too feert tae gie a smile
Nae sillar for a flycup, tae mak her trip worthwhile
Bit lady luck wis on her side, twa hikers up fae Keith
Hid found ma mithers glesses, as weel's a pair o smilin teeth!

The contents o her handbag, were gaithered up in aa
Gweed job it wis the Simmer time, nae twa three feet o snaa!
It surely wis a memorable day, lessons learnt on iss trip?
Keep glesses yokit tae a chyne, an use ultra polygrip!

Caroline Fowler

Where Will the Owls Go Now?

Native English trees at the top of the garden
giants
where owls roost
handkerchief in torchlight
cry when you get out of the car
and know you are home.

when I came back from the edge
where refugees were slumped in corridors of Krakow airport

I want to know where the owls will go.
where blue yellow flags flashed from screens
where we counted the drive-time to the frontline and

Did they know what was happening?
where we scrolled for pictures of people
rescuing pets
– that gunman
with his fish in a square bowl, cat on his back –

Were there nests?
when I came home
and saw you had cut down all the trees

Emily White

Where Truth Lives

Truth lives in what we see.
Not what we want to see.
Most often what we don't want to see, is the truth
The truth isn't forgiveness or light.
The truth is what we force ourselves not to see or believe
The truth is ugly and hurtful

However, the harsh truth is necessary
It's the thing grounding us to reality, and human nature.
Our instinct to know the truth
Not what we want to be the truth.
We ignore the problems facing our species.
We don't want it to be true
Because the truth is ugly and hurtful

Charis Connell

*This poem won third prize in the under 18 category
of the Brian Nisbet Award 2019*

We are Dragons

I am fire,
The wind within the trees,
The freezing snow upon the hills,
The gentle stream below my feet,
The pounding rain however fleet,
It runs through my veins,
The wildness,
The strength,
The gentle grace,
The floating elegance,
And the thundering rage,
For hurt I shall bite,
For I am women,
And we are Dragons,
And we shall fight.

Kerin Muir

Tae a Herrin *(after 'To A Mouse' by Robbie Burns)*

Wee, slith'ry, shiny, ily beastie
O, fit a bonny silv'ry breistie!
Ye need na sweem awa sae hasty
Aye frantic'lly roamin!
Oor boaties nets are sure tae catch ye
Fan feastin, at gloamin.

Ill-trickit craiturs ye maun be
In shoals ye choked oor caul North Sea
Fae Shetland doon tae Yarmouth quay
O, little did ye ken
Ma bonny Silver Darlins
Ye'd meet wi briny eyn.

Peer fishies, sharp knives hid ye hack'it
Sixty a meenit, packit, stackit
Yon fisher lassies, gutted, saat'it
Barrels full't, tae the breem
Quines, clooties row't roon fing-errs, chappit
Hard work, wis life's young dream.

Still, quairter watters furls frothy foam
Ye shimmer, glimmer, noo free tae roam
Still, fisher-men fish, wi nets div comb
Ilka boatie skippered
Wee herrin, tho yer smoked or cured
Yer weel, an truly, kippered!

Caroline Fowler

Summer Tea-Times

Aunt Ella was a lady.
She'd invite her friends for tea.
Her home-made scones were a legend
And as dainty as can be.

Uncle John was a tall man
With the appetite of three.
He'd fit a scone into each cheek
And hope she wouldn't see.
Then hamster-like he'd sit there
With a child upon each knee.

He did this to amuse us,
Of that I am quite sure.
He was a naughty child at heart.
'Twas part of his allure.

Aunt Ella was not fooled by him.
She was a wise old bird.
She'd overlook his childish pranks,
Though thought them quite absurd.

Posh friends did not think much of him,
In all honesty and truth.
They thought he was a foolish man
With manners quite uncouth.

To us he was a hero.
What more is there to tell?
He was our own Pied Piper
And Saint Christopher as well.

Jennifer Rae

The Sunbeam And The Rainbow

'You shine so bright', the Rainbow said
The Sunbeam dazzled quietly

'You shimmer with light' the Sunbeam said
The Rainbow quivered knowingly

And hence they shine and shimmer so
Betwixt and between the bright blue sky and
The thunderous clouds that go scudding by

The sheets of rain that soak all in sight
And the darkest shadows of the darkest night

Between the clouds and the stormy skies
We fleetingly glimpse their stunning surprise

The Sunbeam's smile and the Rainbow's dream
From an Earthly perspective a magical team

And in our hearts, the image remains
Shining and shimmering between the rain
Beating and growing, till we glow and shine

Our lives changed; instantly, silently, lovingly...

Carol Ann

Old Toads and Young

the toads of august
held us in thrall
dusky as crickets
fearfully small
tiptoe, tiptoe
and step with care
we cried to anyone
rambling there

september toadlets
cinnamon buff
as big as twopence
or near enough
struggle aside
as I slash and mow
how I wish I'd
not frightened them so

old toad dreaming
of glories past
I dived so deep
I swam so fast
this earthly carcass
will be my bane
what wouldn't I give
to have gills again

Annie Lamb

Museum

Curious hands caress glass and stone
a cautious touch of fingertip
slow
gentle
run
from
edge
to edge
from gallery to gallery we move
slower than life
adding more steps to this curious dance
a languid tease of gentle loving contact
with unfeeling recipients
gentle attention
contact of warm skin to cold stone
metal and glass
flesh to marble and bronze
polished to lustrous sheen with a thousand affectionate strokes
all performed with hushed reverence
breathed whispers
soft tones
our touch to that unresponsive sculpted skin
compulsion
a transient bond between blood
and the bloodless

Dawn McLachlan

Master Time

in the orchid time
the high light takes a fine
burin to scribe each leaf
a squirrel-hair strokes in
a bee's chinwhiskers

but in the time of asphodel
out comes the hog's hair
the brassy air lays down
broad hollows, hot blue pines
brown butterflies

and in apple time
cold sunlight
sharp-toothed carver of spheres
bronzes the tasty curves
where the wasps hide

but in the time of birches
silverpoint
wielded by high cloud
nowhere hints at the goat moth
in the sapwood

Annie Lamb

Jist Ramblin

Johnny Cash he waak'd the line, richt throu his ring o fire
Patsy Cline gied unco crazy at the muckin o Geordie's byre!

Noo, Charlie Pride wis swingin fae his crystal chandeliers
Peggy Sue left Buddy Holly greetin, in the Valley o tears.

Wi her coat o mony colours Dolly worked fae 9 tae 5
Listenin tae the Rubettes sing aboot yon juke box jive.

The winner takes it all, sang Abba, aye bit fit o aa the losers?
Andy Stewart spiered at Mr Trump: Donald, far's yer troosers?

Tammy Wy-nette she stood b' her man, syne D.I.V.O.R.C.E.
Aa' the Beatles hid tae say wis Help, an let it be!

Nae widden hairt hid Elvis, he's still ayewis on ma mind
Billy Joel found his uptown girl, she wis jist anither kyn.

Queen tuned intae Radio Ga Ga, nae tae K.C.R. like me
Weel a'body kent that Freddie ayewis wintit tae brak free!

Now, it was NOT unusual, Tom Jones he liked tae roam
But aye tae him ere's nithin like the green, green grass of home.

An fit o Steak an Kidney? Aye, oor Sydney, maist Devine
Tho mony fowk micht disagree, he's a Legend in es time.

Daniel Francis Noel o'Donnell sings o bonny Galway Bay
He's a favourite wi the wifies, tae them, Daniel rules, OK?

Roy Orbison wis runnin scared, he cwidna stop his cryin
A pretty woman wid seen cheer him up, o at ere's nae denyin.

Shakin Stevens liked his Green Door, bit he wis taen aback
Fan Mick Jagger fae the Rolling Stones, gart him Paint it Black!

And so tae Lovely Stornoway wi oor favourite Calum Kennedy
That Dark Island is sae bonny, an Outer Hebridean remedy.

Ach weel a've rambled lang aneuch o singers and o sang
Sae a'll sign aff wi the Rollers, an jist say Shang-a-Lang!

Caroline Fowler

In Search of Blind Summit

Is there any sign of Blind Summit?
I've sought him now for weeks on end
Over many long miles of country roads
His absence drives me round the bend

He gives you warning he's ahead
But when you crest the rise
He's nowhere to be seen
Just empty road and empty skies

He has a cousin, this I know,
Blind Pugh, a nasty drunken sot.
Is it he who's changed Blind Summit
To an accident Black Spot?

Leon Stelmach

Ground

In the end, he says:
it's all in the preparation.
I look down at the soil,
two square yards
beyond the compost-heap,
my first ever garden,
pegged and strung
stone-raked Sussex crumb.
His hands spread wide, tools enough,
tanned leather, veined and
calloused by toil. My hands
freshly mulched, fingernails
black crescent moons.
Just scratching the surface,
ten, pink and green.
How do you know
what seed to sow, I ask.
He fans a dozen seed packets:
Up to you, he says.

Bernard Briggs

This poem won 3rd prize in the Brian Nisbet Poetry Award 2021

Field of Dreams

Between deep sleep and waking
A time of reverie and dreaming
What will it be?
Do we choose?

Arms outstretched, jump off a cliff
Soaring high, smiling wide, senses acute;
The plaintive call of a skylark above,
A patchwork of green and gold,
With silver ribbons below.

The buzz of bees collecting pollen,
Rainbow coloured fields of wild flowers,
Field vole rustling through long grass,
Sheer ecstasy; sheer bliss.

And then they come; first one,
Then two, then more;
Vast steel pylons striding cross the land
Deadly cables and glittering balls
Keep your head down.

Soaring no more, frustration;
The unreachable blue, visible beyond;
Forced landing.

Between deep sleep and waking
A time of reverie and dreaming
What will it be?
What will you choose?

Carol Ann

Geordie

Geordie wis an afa loon, ye cwidna get nane rocher
Peer lad ayewis hid a hoast, twis fit ye'd ca a pyocher.

His raivelt dottled Granny, wid yark his sark sae ticht
She lo'ed the laddie dearly, an aye tried tae keep him richt.

Ae dreich an mochie aifterneen, fin Geordie wis real scunnert
Oot stravaigin he did gyang, ower countryside he wannert.

Great plumps o rain cam dingin doon, peer Geordie seen did
    hyter
Noo sypin weet, grun sweelt wi dubs, gied doon wi sic a skylter!

Syne lat oot a scraich, "A've blaud ma breeks, they've turn't a
    fyachie broon
Mither'll gie me sic a row!" Fit a nickum o a loon!

Skweel work wis a tyauve ye see, ach he'd swick fin deein sums
Oor Geordie wid far raither be ootside playin wi his chums.

Teachers were left fusionless, iss bairn wis contermacious
Forfochen wi his cairry-ons, ill-trickit, fyles richt fashious.

Nae formulae for Chemistry, inside oor Geordie's jotter
Jist scoored-oot wark fae start tae eyn, michty, fit a sotter!

He'd stap es pooch wi potions, clarty kirns o smelly stuff
The eyn result wis bowkin, ye'd cowk, for fit a guff!

Weel, that wis mony 'ear ago, fowk thocht he wis a waster
Bit Geordie got the last lauch, for, he's noo the schools
        Heid-Maister!

Caroline Fowler

The Effect of Choice

I think perhaps that I could walk
the mile from my house to the shop,

but then I think of the journey
back, uphill, with the stuff I'd bought.

I wonder, though, if I might enjoy
the sun or if it might rain.

I wonder if I might see trees
blooming; someone in their garden.

I wonder if I might see
a rising butterfly and recall

how its wings cause hurricanes.
And I have no choice after all.

Ian Atkin

This poem was Highly Commended in the Brian Nisbet Poetry Award 2021

Dolphin Spring

1

Ower whaleback hills we loup
greenfingert intae the hert o spring
 an watch the river run the gauntlet o the sea
drainin tae the last peaty drap an dribble
 throu the chalky fingers o the lichthoose.
Ayont the harbour the city humps
an iley shooder tae the warld

2

Ower whaleback hills we loup
greenfingert intae the hert o spring
an watch swack waves furl, dolphin-tailed,
throu saat tides streamin tae the finny brink
skelpin flukes o airy spume tae the halleyracket win.
Bi the harbour waa shags salute
a stiff-neckit parade o eider duck

Linda Smith

Cosmic Rainbow Dragon

It started as a speck of light,
A distant star in the night-time sky.
It caught my eye, twinkling as it did,
Demanding to be noticed, it wasn't shy.

The speck of light then grew and grew
The colour changed, a rainbow hue.
It danced across the Milky Way,
A splash of light that appeared on cue.

Each night I looked for the bouncing light,
Each night it grew till rainbows filled the sky.
Each day I wondered what it was
That shone so bright, so vividly.
And then it burst, a million rainbows,
Gently floating, gently dancing on the breeze.

One appeared in my garden, yesterday
I saw it briefly out the corner of an eye
as I turned away;
Playing between the dragon yews and the fairy hole
Hiding, tantalisingly, in plain sight.

And as I watched, it landed on my hand
A tiny dragon of vivid, pearlescent hue
Observing me, closely,
as I smiled and said 'hello'.
I felt it jump into my heart;
It lies there still; waiting, quietly.
And I am now a part,
of the Cosmic Rainbow Dragon.

Carol Ann

Birth Day

I see you,
fresh to the world
with weak legs
and knobbly knees,
cloak of womb
still clinging
as you stumble
towards weary sustenance,
becoming cocooned
and washed
by maternal love.
A new day, a new season.
Welcome, little lamb.

Anne Manning

A Single Raven Flying North

man, throw down a bone
a sticky red bone
and on the bald slope
I'll spy it

gralloch your kill
by the snowmelt stream
I'll sip cold silver
unpick the secret coils

the warrior is gone and the wolf
and no more provender
falls from their careless blade
and generous fang

along the beach where once
weapons were thirsty and the sand
drank blood, no more the dead
only a whistling man sports with the gale

man, throw a salute
to me your brother
wind-rider and snatcher of spoils
we know the meaning of bones

Annie Lamb

Have You Ever?

Have you ever rested
on a carpet of blue
as sunlight filtered
through velvet buds
while birds nested
and lambs called
to a mother's love?
Have you ever stopped
interrupted
by a cuckoo's song
sent gently
along the breeze
silencing
endless busy thoughts?
Have you ever stood
barefoot
on sunrise grass
toes curling
dew to skin
birds calling
to a brand new day?
Have you ever watched
in awe
the swallows dance
red flashes
with forked tails
playing chase
against evening skies?

Have you ever had
a thirst
for icy air
in stale lungs
when frost tipped grass
capped by fallen leaves
beckons you outside?
Have you ever seen
roosting crows
settle
amongst golds and yellows,
as woodsmoke threads
across the setting sun
of a lean day?
Have you ever felt
the Northern wind
work it's fingers
between scarf and hat
skin tingling and eyes watering
but spirit warmed
by a hearth's promise?
Have you ever walked
under a waning moon
on crunching snow,
torch light catching
sparkling grasses
as branches lean
towards exhaled air?

Have you ever wondered
at the multitude of moments
marking time's passing
collected across the years
grounding us
to our place in life
and the world around us?
I have.

Anne Manning

How Do We Not See

How do we not see
What is right in front of us
Blind to ever rising seas
Slow cooking of earth's crust

Blurred view of humanity
Equality slides on unbalanced scales
Myopic glances, our vanity
Missing other's intricate details

How do we not see
The light dimming upon us
Is obtuse a new way to be
Or, always superfluous
... were we

Elizabeth Mccarthy

This poem was Highly Commended in the Brian Nisbet Poetry Award 2020

I've Lost Truth

I've lost truth; I've left it somewhere lying
Maybe in an old book or photo of my dad
I don't know.
I've mislaid truth, it's somewhere hiding
Maybe in a past memory or in a trunk in the attic
I can't remember anymore.
They say truth will out
But I'm still waiting.

Nick May

This poem won third prize in the Brian Nisbet Award 2019

Passin fit-steps

A sat in quairt reflection cassen een doon at the fleer
The soun o passin fit-steps wis aa that I cwid hear
Fowk gaan waukin back an fore, weerin diff'rent kines o sheen
Ma thochts seen turn't tae windrin fit the styles o them micht mean.

Mannies polished Balmoral's, weel turn't oot an smert
Fairmers sharny dubby beets jist hame fae the mairt
Young quines skippin by me wi a pair o coaties on
Trainers for swack joggers oot tae rin a mar-a-thon.

Dainty satin ballet slippers, deein a pas de bas
A dame trips ower stiletto heels tryin sair nae tae faa!
Shauchlin cosy baffies shufflin slowly wi great care
Flappin flimsy flip-flops, peelie-wally leggies bare.

Comfy sheen the verra dunt for busy workin mums
Trendy up-tae-date anes, fin oot for a lauch wi chums
Steel tae caps note for workin men, far safety's gien a boost
"Follow me", smiles Uncle Johnny, "an yer tackits'll nivver roost."

Sparkly stylish sling-backs, maun be aff tae a fancy doo
Hale-gran fan-toosh dressy anes, heidin oot for a Vindaloo
The mairchin beat o Army beets strictly keepin time
Elegant Bobby Dazzlers pittin on the Ritz tae dine.

Ivvery day weerin anes fin hingin oot yer claes
Welly beets keep oot the weet on plowtery dreich like days
Wi sterile crocs the surgeon's deein life-savin ops
The wrang kine says e hirplin wife, stravaigin roon ower muckle shops!

Winkle Pickers, Brothel Creepers dancin feet o Rock an Roll
Dirt deen weariet Miners, black beets, black lungs, black coal
Sae handsome wis the kilted Groom, ghillie brogues full o style
His Bonny Bride wauks-on-air, heid-ower-heels up the aisle.

Sturdy durable hill-waukin beets for climmin craggy Munros
Scottish Country dancin pumps perform at Hielan Shows
Prosthetic sheen are custom made, for heroic amputees
Fly fisher-men Don waders that gyang hyne abeen their knees.

Street urchins ga'an aboot barfit, it's grim they hinna sheen
Hairy fittit werewolves? Jist fowk dressed up at Hallow'een.
Easy faisten'd velcro anes, fit bairns at nursery weer
Primary1, his first school sheen, time tae shed a tear.

Elevated platforms, some reach an afa heicht
A doot a maun be gettin auld, for michty, fit a sicht!
Youngsters wi yon jeelie kine, paddlin in the cauld North Sea
Auld scuddlin jimmies jist the job for sclimmin up thon tree.

Nurses practical white anes, seein tae patients on the ward
Same kine for the midwife as she cuts the umbilical cord
Babies knitted bootees, happin ten wee tiny taes
Sandals wi a cushioned sole, pyowin awa in Simmer days.

Strong reliable lacin anes, for Bobbies on the beat
Ony kine that gyang on easy-osily, fan a wheelchair is yer seat
Scruffy, filthy worn deen sheen, fit's been their tale tae tell?
A winner his their earthly life jist been pure livin Hell?

Court shoes, as the lawyer tries anither harrowin case
Loafers for the laid back fowk, daunerin at a slower pace
Grassy covered fitba beets, loons aim tae score some goals
The Minister prays: "Oor Faither, please forgie, an save oor Souls."

A taen a deep breath in, syne gied oot a great lang sigh
Iss worl is full o different fowk, aa jist passin by
An lookin doon a winnert, shid a lauch oot loud or greet
At ma ain bauchled sheen, an twa muckle bappy feet!

Caroline Fowler

Today

I heard crackling today
of Broom's black seed pods,
threatening to burst
and disperse
under a hot sun,
the vanilla smell
of yellow flowers
gone but lingering
in memory.
I heard rustling
of feathered Barley,
their golden heads bent
longingly
towards wild rosehips
and faded willowherb
while butterflies fluttered
spoilt for choice
between.
I heard the stridulation.
of lonely grasshoppers,
their songs of love
carried through heavy air
amplified by
the silence of birds
under shade.

I heard the tired scrape
of footsteps on hard earth,
that led to a creaking gate
reluctant to open wide
into flowering meadows
and welcoming paths
towards home.

Anne Manning

Catching Time

My hands caught time without me realising
The years crept across them leaving freckled footprints
brown pressed on paper-thin
tissue-like, drawn tight
Decades pasted upon knuckle bones
The lines of palm that in my youth
were sharp, and deep
and spoke of truth
of future hopes and things to come
now speak more of years long gone
A craquelure of wet
and cold
and faster years
and growing old
When I was small and pink of fist
with life to come and nothing missed
my grandmother's stern hands reigned
Oven-red, bleach-sore
sausage-fingered, berry-stained
white and sweet with flour and sugar
rose-scratched, earthy raw
steadying and strong
At her bedside as the lights of her life dimmed
I saw the tissue of her skin
thin-laced over knotted bones
pulse stutter
Her grip a mere moth-like flutter

I laid my hands over hers as she neared a century old
and wondered if she'd felt the years unfold
if she, in her time, had also thought
of all the years her hands had caught
and if she had mused on how much they
had accidentally let slip away.

Dawn McLachlan

This poem won first prize in the Brian Nisbet Poetry Award 2019

A Chorus of Crocuses

Turning the corner from
winter's dull browns and greys,
vast carpets of purple and white
 meet my smiling gaze.

Bursting through the rust
of last year's leaves
Reaching for the Sun
on sturdy stalks of green
Beautiful crocus,
the essence of Spring.

And as the warming sun
shines through the trees
Closed petals open,
and orange hearts zing.

Sighs and smiles, drinking
the colours on the breeze
A chorus of crocuses
to make the heart sing.

Carol Ann

There Are Many Words for Beauty

If a boy's skin
is too thin
to keep his beauty in

and rages
cracks and breaks,
the worlds says

why are his teeth so big
why are his toes so small
clack clack

There are many words for beauty:

his bones under it
arch like ballet
over the sides of the world

Emily White

Too Busy Dancin

Twis ma choice tae ging doon the chute,
the een at the open air pool.
The yalla moo gawpit, 'Come awa...'
Yer nae a bairn noo, ye aul feel!

Twis oor final Aqua Zumba fling
Aa the ravers hid flooers n their hair,
winkin an twerkin wi the lifeguard loons
fa kint aa the lithe moves, fit rare.

Skirls o 'Seonaidh, can ye handle this?'
splashes o deco turquoise.
We're aa Destiny's chiels, noo
'shak yer money-maker...' feel the noise.

I wisna aleen, ither wifies lined up
unner the michty steps shimmies
aa shapes n sizes o dowp, scalin
the stairway n rip curl jimmies.

The skelfie afore me fair shot doon
gaen her heedie a clatterin dunt
she slippit richt aneth the watter
An fleggit aabody, exeunt.

But up she bobbit, jist wavin nae droonin,
black affrontit. My shottie on the chute.
Watter tricklit doon, still shakkin
I thocht that I micht chicken oot

Wis it choice tae hurl mysel forward?
Or wis't fear o freezin fast?
Plunged an purged, we emerged gypin,
Trickit, summer selkies at last.

Nicola Furrie Murphy

*This poem won second prize for a Doric poem
in the Brian Nisbet Poetry Award 2021*

A Thing o Beauty?

Weel, pollyfilla fills the cracks o wrinkles on ma broo
Thin silver threids upon ma heid far gowden hair aince grew
Ers nithin beats a twa three dabs o richt strong super glue
The verra dunt for keepin shooglie falsers in ma moo!

A've haen tae taen tae shuvin in yon chicken fillets noo
Mither Naitur startit heidin Sooth, an gie near oot o view!
A badly need mair beauty sleep, nae jist an oor or two
Am up at scraich o day tae dicht ma face wi sparklin dew!

Dist mak a diff'rence? Nae one bit, it's jist the same aul me
Ower mony fowk get sookit in, glamourie products on T.V.
A've tae clart on umpteen lotions, nae fae a beautician
I'm laden doon wi Chemist's bags, full o ammunition!

Fyachy creams for my Rosacea, ach yon's nae a bonny sicht
It looks nae bad hoo-ivver in the gloamin at twilicht!
Nae need tae pit the blusher on, ma face is ayewis reed
I'm sure fowk think a've weet ma thrapple howpin Amber Bead!

Voltarol Gel gets rubbit in, aa roon ma arthritic knee
Syne rowed wi fyangles o' bandages as ticht as they kin be
Pink peels a hae tae swallae, tryin tae help fit gies me jip
Aye, the nivver-eynin stoonin fae ma crumblin, hirplin hip!

Nae fancy painted polished nails, aa bonny manicured
They'd jist get in the wye, fan tae the gairden I am lured
Fa cwid get the weedin deen, wi muckle talons powkin oot?
Forbyes ma bappy fing-errs wid look daft athoot a doot!

Nah! Moisturizin cream seeps intae roch an chappit hans
Wi skin sae paper thin noo, nae ile paintin o Cezanne's
A stowff aboot in bauchled, tho richt comfy, worn-in sheen
They've trodden mony places fancy high heels hinna seen.

Ma bat wings keep on flappin, the bairns aye hae a lauch
Wobblin the Magnificat, by Jo-hann Sebastian Bach!
Aye, beauty's only skin deep, we learn as we get older
Thankfully subjective and, in the een o the beholder.

Caroline Fowler

The gas station, or: choice, what choice?

high summer rain
car full of kids
she's never stopped here before
she pulls in
and they all see it
puppies for sale five bucks
regular she says, fill her up
I guess your dogs are in there
old wooden barrel stuffed with straw
long dark nose questing out
shepherds she says

well says the lady holding the nozzle
their father ain't

and the rain rumbles down on the concrete
the lady's slicker, the barrel, the car
the pup – what's he doin' out in the rain?
he's just a runt, says the lady
tothers keep kickin' him out

she tells them later he won't get big
round and round on the dining room rug
his feet are small
the kids believe her
when has she ever been wrong?

Annie Lamb

This poem was highly commended in the Brian Nisbet Award 2021

About Huntly Writers

This volume of poetry has been predominantly written by members of the Huntly Writers. We are a group of writers from all walks of life and our home group was founded in the rural market town of Huntly in Aberdeenshire, Scotland. Huntly Writers is an unincorporated association of writers, which raises its own funding for the most part, with occasional help from the Scottish Book Trust with readings and workshops. We exist to support local writers by providing regular sessions where they can read their work and receive constructive criticism from fellow members. The group also arranges readings and workshops by established authors. In previous years, public performances of our work have taken place once or twice a year and we have regular collaborations with other writers and artists. We also publish anthologies of our work, one of which you hold in your hand.

For more information about Huntly Writers, biographical details of the poets in this book and for details of how to contact poets individually, please see our website:

www.huntly-writers.co.uk

The Brian Nisbet Poetry Award

Brian Nisbet was an Aberdeenshire based poet, musician and academic who had strong connections to Huntly and the Huntly Writers. Brian died in 2015 aged 56 of the neurological disorder multiple system atrophy (MSA). He is greatly missed by his readers and by those who knew and loved him.

His poetry collection "Now You Know" celebrated all that Brian found life-enhancing (including his own beloved spaniel, Juno) but never hid what his illness meant to him both physically and emotionally. His poem "The Naming of Symptoms" (after Henry Reed) was shortlisted in 2014 by Parkinson's UK for a Mervyn Peake award. "Now Your Know" was accepted by the Poetry Library in London for its reference collection.

In Brian's memory there exists the annual Brian Nisbet Poetry Award. This is launched with a theme subject every autumn and many of the winners' poems are contained within this collection.

Brian's wife, the musician Emily White, is also an accomplished poet and a member of the Huntly Writers. You can find several of her poems in this book.

For more information about the Brian Nisbet Poetry Award please search for their page on Facebook.